D1355737

ANNE HOOPER'S

POCKET SEX GUIDE

A DORLING KINDERSLEY BOOK

First published in Great Britain in 1994
by Dorling Kindersley Limited,
9 Henrietta Street, London WC2E 8PS
Copyright © 1994 Dorling Kindersley Limited, London

Reprinted 1996

Created and produced by
CARROLL & BROWN LIMITED
5 Lonsdale Road
London NW6 6RA

Editor Amy Carroll
Art Editor Alan Watt

Photographers Ranald MacKechnie
Paul Robinson
Artwork Howard Pemberton

A CIP catalogue record for this book is available from the
British Library.

ISBN 0 7513 0089 6

Reproduced by Colourscan, Singapore
Printed and bound in Great Britain

introduction
4-6

chapter one
THE EXPERT LOVER
7-26

chapter two
FANTASTIC FOREPLAY
27-54

chapter three
VARIATIONS ON MAKING LOVE
55-95

index
96

introduction

A recent television programme showed that only 21 per cent of men tested actually knew the whereabouts of the clitoris. This must have been devastating for the partners of the other 79 per cent. More importantly, it established that there is a profound link between sexual knowledge and the ability to be a rewarding and sensual lover.

Similarly, women asking for help with non-achievement of orgasm invariably know nothing of their own sexual responses. When women learn what their anatomy consists of and how their sexuality works, they, more often than not, become orgasmic. The instant result is that they grow more confident and their lovers have more fun.

But becoming a good lover requires more than a knowledge of sexual anatomy and sexual response. It implies a sense of comfort with matters sexual, and

an open appreciation of new
ideas and suggestions.
Reaching this degree of
comfort usually involves
talking about sex, reading
about sex, and looking
at interesting
pictures – in short,
learning to be open about a
subject that has traditionally been a very private one.

A pocket book is, by its very nature, a book that can
be carried around, treated casually, dipped into, passed
to friends, and studied and appreciated with a partner.
Because it is small, a pocket guide is less intimidating
than a large tome but instead allows us to treat the
subject with ease.

There has been a long tradition of pocket sex books
– laughed at and played with by lovers for many
hundreds of years. The ancient Japanese studied them
with intensity, the Victorians with surreptitiousness,
and the Edwardians with a joke
and a twirl of the
moustache.

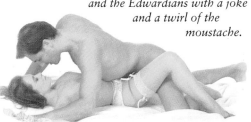

*This, our present-day
version, offers you
beautiful bodies,
entwined in the artistic
shapes of love. As a
miniature feast for the
eyes, we hope it both pleases
you and provides food for
fantasy and the imagination.
On a practical level,
these pages are packed with
pictorial information. If you
take this little volume to
bed with you, there can be
no excuses for boredom or
for heavy handedness. Please
bear in mind that the hands, and
the tongue are our most sensuous
tools of lovemaking and that the brain, with its far-
ranging ability to create ideas and pictures, the most
vital erotic organ of all. This little book, therefore,
has been invented to stimulate your imagination. I
sincerely hope it enriches many hundreds of spring
nights, summer afternoons, autumn evenings, and
winter mornings with your lover.*

Anne Hooper

chapter one

THE EXPERT
LOVER

SEXUAL RESPONSE

While men and women differ in what arouses them and the time it takes for them to become aroused, the stages of response are identical.

FEMALE RESPONSE
This takes longer to develop but lasts longer than in the male, and is more easily rekindled.

AROUSAL
With foreplay, the vagina grows in length and becomes lubricated. The cervix and the uterus are pulled backwards and upwards, and the inner and outer labia enlarge. She is ready to be penetrated.

The vagina becomes moist and the clitoris enlarges

The breasts swell and the nipples become erect

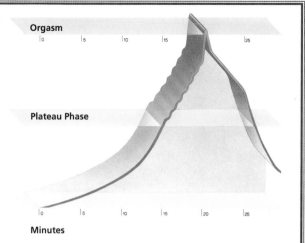

Orgasm

| 0 | 5 | 10 | 15 | | 25 |

Plateau Phase

| 0 | 5 | 10 | 15 | 20 | 25 |

Minutes

ORGASM

A woman's orgasm depends on the amount of stimulation her clitoris receives, either from penile thrusting or from manual or oral manipulation. From the plateau phase, her sexual tension intensifies until it culminates in a peak of pleasurable orgasmic contractions.

RESOLUTION

Over a period of 10-15 minutes, the pleasurable feelings ebb and the swollen clitoris and labia contract in size. If stimulation is resumed, however, some women may be able to achieve further orgasms.

MALE RESPONSE

This develops more quickly but is of a shorter duration than a female's. Moreover, orgasm is inevitable if a man is sufficiently aroused.

AROUSAL
Once a man is turned on, signals from the brain travel down the spinal cord to the genitals and send blood flowing into the penis, thus ensuring erection. His normally limp, downward-hanging organ, is replaced by a rigid, upward-thrusting, throbbing one, the scrotum is drawn up closer to the body, and the testes thicken.

Heart and breathing rates increase and blood pressure rises

Increased blood supply leads to reddening and mottling of the skin

Nipple swelling and erection may occur

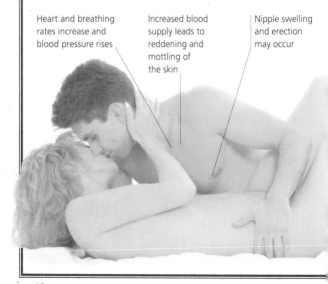

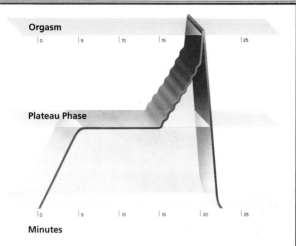

Orgasm

| 0 | 5 | 10 | 15 | | 25 |

Plateau Phase

| 0 | 5 | 10 | 15 | 20 | 25 |

Minutes

ORGASM

A man can remain at a plateau of sensation until he penetrates his partner. Once he does so, his sexual tension quickly intensifies as he thrusts until his climax forces the urethra and penile muscles to contract and ejaculate semen. Climax is usually intensely pleasurable.

DETUMESCENCE

After ejaculation, the penis becomes flaccid and a man's arousal level plummets. Most men enter a period, variable in duration, in which further erections are not possible.

MALE SEX ORGANS

The visible sex organs are the penis and scrotum. Inside the scrotum are the testes (testicles) and the epididymides, where sperm are produced and stored. Internal organs include the prostate gland, vas deferens, and the seminal vesicles.

The sensitive glans (head) of the penis is packed with nerve endings

The frenulum, on the underside of the penis where the glans meets the shaft, is very sensitive

THE PENIS

The major organ of sexual intercourse, the average unerect penis is 9.5 cms (3 3/4 in) long. With sexual stimulation, the interior blood vessels fill and cause it to swell and become erect, and capable of penetration.

CIRCUMCISION

A man may have his foreskin surgically removed for reasons of religion or hygiene. Contrary to popular myth, a circumcised man does not experience either a heightened or reduced sensitivity during sex, nor is his ability to control ejaculation affected in any way.

Uncircumcised

Circumcised

Seminal Vesicle
There are two seminal vesicles, one each side of the bladder. They produce the sticky seminal fluid, which, together with sperm, forms the ejaculate.

Vas Deferens
Two tubes that carry sperm from the epididymides to the seminal vesicles prior to ejaculation.

Prostate Gland
Within this fibrous organ, ducts from the seminal vesicles join the urethra. Manual stimulation of the gland can produce exquisite orgasms.

Scrotum
This is a pouch of skin that covers both testes. Under the skin is a layer of muscle that contracts and draws the testes up towards the groin.

Testis
One of two smooth, oval organs whose function is to produce sperm and male hormones such as testosterone.

FEMALE SEX ORGANS

The vulva is the most accessible part of a woman's sex organs and is comprised of the clitoris, labia minora and majora, and the vaginal opening. It is highly individual to each woman in terms of appearance and sensitivity.

THE CLITORIS

This is the most erotically sensitive part of a woman's body; it contains abundant nerve endings that make it extremely sensitive to stimulation. Direct clitoral stimulation with the fingers, tongue, or penis is usually the only way most women will achieve orgasm.

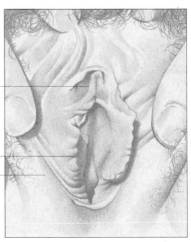

Clitoris
About 2-3 cm long and bent back on itself, during sexual excitement it doubles in size and becomes erect.

Labia Minora
The inner lips produce sebum that helps to lubricate the vagina during sexual arousal.

Labia Majora
These outer lips contain sebaceous and apocrine glands; the latter produce a sexually attractant odour.

THE VAGINA

This fibro-muscular tube measures approximately 8 cms (3 1/2 in) long on average, but with sexual excitement expands in length and diameter to accommodate any size of penis with ease. When a woman is sufficiently aroused, the vagina is lubricated with a milky fluid. During orgasm, the vaginal walls contract and grip the penis; this results in extremely pleasurable sensations for both partners.

Pubic bone
During intercourse, this presses the penis down on to the clitoris, so producing stimulation.

Urethra
This 4-cm (1 1/2 in) tube through which urine is excreted from the bladder exits just in front of the vagina.

Cervix
This, the head of the vagina, projects into the vaginal opening, dividing it into front, back and lateral fornices.

Vagina
The lining is thick and is formed into prominent folds that run horizontally and vertically.

THE G-SPOT

Said to be an internal erogenous zone, this is an area of nerve endings, ducts, glands, and blood vessels. Although it is not normally discernible, during deep vaginal stimulation it swells, and in some women produces very pleasurable feelings.

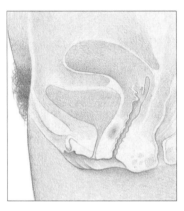

WHERE IT IS
The G-spot was "discovered" by German gynaecologist, Ernst Grafenburg, on the vagina's front wall. While it appears to be a super-sensitive area for some women, not all find their G-spots easily, and some solo or shared exploration may be necessary.

STIMULATING THE G-SPOT
With your partner sitting or lying back, insert a finger into her vagina and use it to press the front wall about two-thirds of the way up. The G-spot should swell when you touch it.

G-SPOT STIMULATION DURING SEX

Any position in which there is sustained pressure on the front wall of the vagina is good for G-spot stimulation. Woman-on-top positions are particularly effective because the woman can control the depth of penetration. Rear-entry positions are also good because of the angle at which the penis penetrates the vagina. The man should help by moving his body and controlling his penis so that its head makes contact with the G-spot.

You are free to move back and forth or to the side to maintain pressure on this pleasurable area

You may experience an intense orgasm if your G-spot is stimulated sufficiently by your partner

Concentrate on keeping your penis in contact with the front wall of the vagina rather than moving around continuously

SAFER SEX

Sexual practices that prevent the passage of bodily fluids between partners protect against the transmission of HIV infection, AIDS, and other sexually transmitted diseases. Safer sex is usually non-penetrative or performed while using a condom. Unless you are in a steady, long-term monogamous relationship with a partner whose sexual history is known, a condom should be worn.

Both partners can safely indulge in massage, kissing, mutual masturbation, and shared sexual fantasies

emidom

Condoms
Available for both sexes, these prevent contact with a partner's semen or vaginal fluid.

Sheaths

HIGH RISK ACTIVITIES	LOWER RISK ACTIVITIES
•Anal sex without using a condom •Vaginal sex without using a condom •Sharing penetrative sex aids, such as vibrators •Any activity that involves drawing blood, whether intentionally or not •Insertion of fingers into the anus	•Vaginal sex with a condom •Fellatio or cunnilingus using a condom or latex barrier •Deep mouth-to-mouth kissing (you increase the risk if you have bleeding gums or cold sores) •Rubbing genitals against partner's body

USING A CONDOM

In addition to being an efficient form of contraception, a condom will protect against the

spread of sexually transmitted disease. Although often regarded as a "passion killer", it can augment erotic sensation if applied skilfully. Check that the condom you are using is not past its expiry date, and that the packet bears a safety kitemark. Those designed as pleasure enhancers (ribbed, flavoured or shaped condoms) should not be relied on for contraceptive or safer sex purposes.

1 Make sure that your partner has a full erection; a sensuous genital massage will ensure this. Open the foil packet carefully so that you don't damage the condom.

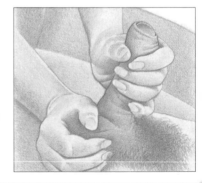

2 Place the unrolled condom on the top of the penis and, using your thumb and forefinger, squeeze out any air from the tip. (During intercourse an air bubble could cause the condom to split.)

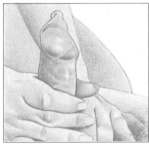

3 Hold the base of your partner's penis in one hand and unroll the condom over it with the other. If he has not been circumcised, push back his foreskin before applying the condom.

4 Once your partner has ejaculated but before his erection has subsided, he should withdraw his penis from your vagina, making sure that he keeps the condom in place by holding on to the rim. Dispose of the condom safely, taking care not to spill any semen.

MALE MASTURBATION

A man can gain a good deal of knowledge about his own sexuality from masturbation. And, if he shares this knowledge with his partner, it will often bring about enhanced mutual satisfaction. Any insights gained regarding sexual behaviour generally contribute to a couple's enjoyment.

EXPERIMENT
Slowly stroke along the length of the shaft, then concentrate on the glans and the frenulum – the most sensitive parts of the penis. Combine this with moving your pelvis up and down in rhythm.

TIME IS OF THE ESSENCE

Many men rush the process and try to get it over with too quickly; this can lead to problems with technique and timing later on. Use slow strokes of differing intensities, and indulge in sexual fantasies.

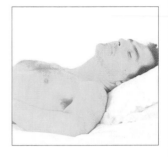

MAKE IT A WHOLE-BODY EXPERIENCE

Include light touching along the length of your body, paying special attention to your most sensitive spots. Lightly run your fingers along your face, and over your nipples, chest, and inner thighs, before stimulating your genitals. Don't be afraid to let yourself go; you shouldn't worry about controlling your breathing or any vocal expressions.

Squeeze your legs together rhythmically and move your thighs up and down for extra sensation

Use a lubricant such as massage oil to make your touch slippery and sensuous

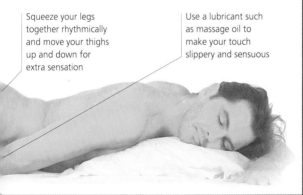

FEMALE MASTURBATION

Before a woman can communicate her sexual needs to a partner, she needs to find them out for herself. Masturbation is the best route to sexual self-discovery and increased pleasure for both.

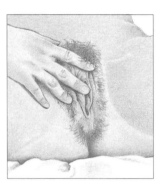

CLITORAL STIMULATION

Some women like to massage the shaft of the clitoris between their fingers, some make circular movements over the whole clitoral area, others use just one finger to lightly brush the top of the clitoris.

LET YOURSELF GO

Allow yourself privacy in which to experiment with pleasurable sensations. Use fantasy to heighten arousal and experiment with touches of different speeds and rhythms, then progress to pelvic thrusting and squeezing your thighs. Movement and sound will contribute to the intensity.

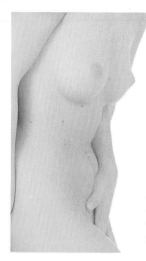

WHOLE-BODY STIMULATION

Start with light strokes over your entire body then increase the pressure and rhythm until you are stimulating your most sensitive spots. Concentrate on the nipples and breasts before moving on to the inner thighs and genitals. Stroke the whole length of the vulva before reaching inside. Then, when sufficiently lubricated, slide your fingers in and around your vagina. Squeeze your thighs together to put more pressure on your genital area.

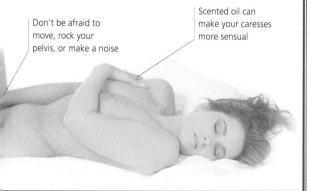

Don't be afraid to move, rock your pelvis, or make a noise

Scented oil can make your caresses more sensual

USING A VIBRATOR

Used mainly by women, a vibrator can produce explosive sensations in those who have some difficulty reaching orgasm from penetrative sex, and can add to the pleasure of both partners. A man can use it to stimulate his partner during sex or can apply it to his penis.

VIBRATORS
These valuable sex aids trigger erotic sensation wherever there are any nerve receptors, most particularly in the genital regions of both sexes.

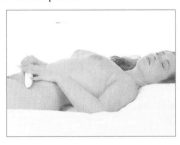

Use the vibrator on the vaginal entrance, the inner thighs, and the perineum, as well as the clitoris

WOMEN AND VIBRATORS
Orgasm is almost guaranteed if a vibrator is used; the sensation may be similar to, or even surpass, that achieved from stimulation by the hand or penis.

chapter two

FANTASTIC FOREPLAY

SEXY UNDRESSING

Visual stimulation can be very arousing and you can add eroticism to sex by undressing provocatively in front of your partner. Similarly, being undressed by a partner is a real turn-on. Take it in turn to be the exhibitionist or the more passive partner. Try wearing underwear that you wouldn't normally wear or that you know your partner likes.

Look away from your partner or turn your back to him to increase eroticism

UNDRESSING YOURSELF

Move your hands very slowly and provocatively over your body. Use languorous movements as you take off each garment.

TAKING TURNS

Always treat your partner sensitively. Kiss and caress her or him as each garment is removed.

Step out of your clothes and leave them lying on the floor

UNDRESSING YOUR PARTNER

Make a game of removing his or her clothes. As you take something off, use it to tease and tantalize your partner.

EROGENOUS ZONES

Areas that can be stimulated to produce erotic sensation exist anywhere on the body from your scalp to your feet. Some of these erogenous zones, such as the lips and breasts, are common to everyone; others are unique to the individual.

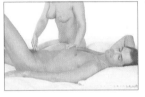

GENITALS
These are the most erogenous parts of the body, containing the largest number of sensual nerve endings.

HEAD AND NECK
Filled with sensory nerve receptors, the lips, neck, and ear lobes are particularly responsive sites.

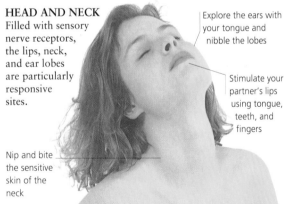

Explore the ears with your tongue and nibble the lobes

Stimulate your partner's lips using tongue, teeth, and fingers

Nip and bite the sensitive skin of the neck

CHEST

The upper part of a man's body, particularly his nipples, will respond pleasurably to stroking and kissing.

BREASTS

The nipples and their areolae are extremely sensitive to touch; the nipples become erect when kissed or sucked. Some women report that nipple stimulation alone can bring them to orgasm. Start off by lightly brushing your partner's nipples with your fingertips, then move on to squeezing and sucking them.

FEET

The feet are often neglected as an erogenous zone. Sucking and massaging the toes is highly erotic. Concentrate on the skin between the toes, the soles, and the arches of the feet. To avoid tickling your partner, move your hands in firm, circular strokes.

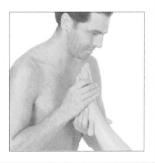

KISSING

A kiss can be a greeting, an expression of love, or an essential part of foreplay. Because the lips and tongue are among the most sensitive parts of the body, deep kissing can be as erotic as sex itself.

MOUTH-TO-MOUTH

The lips, tongue, and the inside of the mouth are all sensitive to stimulation. Vary your kisses so that some are soft and yielding, others hard and demanding.

FRENCH KISSING

Exploring your partner's mouth, tongue, and lips with your tongue creates a mood of intimacy in addition to communicating how sexy you feel. Older, more established, couples sometimes neglect it.

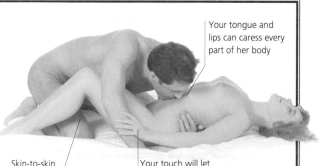

Your tongue and lips can caress every part of her body

Skin-to-skin contact increases sexual arousal

Your touch will let your partner know how you are feeling

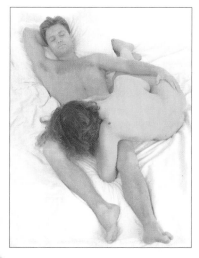

ALL-OVER KISSING
Don't just kiss your partner in the usual places. Use your mouth and tongue along the length of his or her body, including obvious places like the breasts and inner thighs, as well as the more tactile backs of the knees and the fingers.

STROKING AND TOUCHING

Learning to enjoy touching your partner and receiving caresses in exchange is one of the joys of lovemaking. Making an effort to learn about your partner's body, particularly areas that you wouldn't normally consider sexual, such as the hands, arms, feet, and calves, can bring sensual rewards.

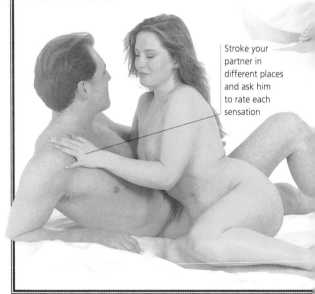

Stroke your partner in different places and ask him to rate each sensation

GUIDE YOUR PARTNER

Instead of telling your partner what you like, put your hand on hers or his, and guide it to where you want to be touched.

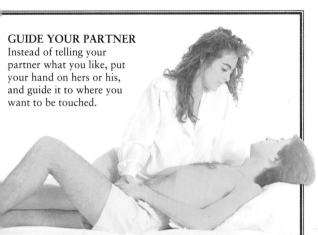

SHARED EXPERIENCES

Be sensitive to your partner's responses and adjust your movements as he or she indicates.

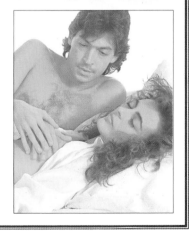

EROTIC ENHANCERS

The intimacy of touch adds to the sexual communication between partners – touching teaches you about your sensual responses as well as those of your partner. A variety of aids can be used to maximize eroticism over the entire body and enhance the range and intensity of touches, and thereby inject variety into lovemaking.

The scalp is sensitive to a range of touches

SOFT-BRISTLED BRUSHES
Languorous brushing of the hair, combined with gentle body strokes, is relaxing and soothing. On bare skin, a soft brush will tickle and stimulate.

EDIBLES

Small fruits, cream, and champagne are some of the treats that can be applied to, dabbed on, or crushed against a partner's body and then eaten, sucked, or licked off. Strategic positioning can increase the eroticism.

MASKS

Hiding your partner's eyes will heighten anticipation; fulfill it with silken caresses. Titillate her or him with unexpected touches.

BODY PAINT

Edible, washable paint is a sensual treat for both partners. It feels as good to dip in your fingers and smear it on your own skin as it does for a partner. Use it to signal your "special" spots.

SENSUAL MASSAGE

Sometimes, desire ebbs and needs to be rekindled or alternatively, partners may crave extended lovemaking. Intimate body contact can enhance sensuality and set the mood and pace for sex. Partners must be relaxed, so make sure that you will not be interrupted and that the room is warm. Undress, and use a scented oil, warmed between your hands, to help smooth your movements.

Concentrate on enjoying the sensations you are experiencing

Adopt a comfortable position; skin-to-skin contact is exciting

Start with gentle, exploratory movements along the length of your partner's body

FEATHERING
Skim your fingertips over your partner's skin very lightly so that he or she can barely feel your touch. You can also use your fingernails very gently. Feathering is particularly sensual on the back.

CIRCLING
Put your palms on your partner's body and move them round and round in a circular motion. This basic massage stroke will warm up and relax the muscles.

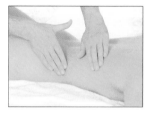

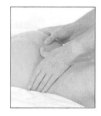

KNUCKLING
Make your hands into a half-fist and use the joints of your fingers or your knuckles to massage your partner's back, buttocks, and legs.

KNEADING AND THUMB PRESSURE
You can unknot tense muscles by squeezing and releasing the flesh in a kneading action. Exert pressure on a particular point by moving your thumbs repeatedly in a small circle.

SHARING A MASSAGE

Take it in turns to be the giving or receiving partner. Begin with a back massage using a variety of strokes, as shown on the previous pages, then move on to the buttocks, thighs, and calves. Pay some attention to the less sexual areas of the body, such as the feet, before massaging the lips, breasts, nipples, and genitals.

Use long or circular strokes on the flanks

Kneading or pummelling works well on fleshy areas

FACE
Use light, feathery touches on the lips, cheeks, and chin and firmer finger pressure on the temples, forehead, and sinus areas.

BODY

Use your whole body to caress all of your partner's. Intimate bodily contact need not be limited to hands – lips, breasts, genitals, even hair, can all be employed.

Covering a partner's body with your own is highly arousing

Vary your movements so they are soft and sensuous or urgent and exciting

FOOT

Start by rubbing lotion into the foot, then use your palm to gently bend the toes upwards; pay attention to the skin in-between each toe. Use your knuckles or the heel of your hand to massage the sole of the foot. Gradually increase your caresses until each stroke lasts the length of the foot; let your hands glide over the surface. Then take the foot in one hand and the lower calf in the other, and rotate the foot gently and slowly several times.

MUTUAL MASTURBATION

Manually stimulating your partner to orgasm can be a fulfilling alternative to penetration: you still have the intimacy of sex and the pleasure of climaxing, but it is completely safe and you have greater control over each other's responses. Find out what your partner enjoys. As you touch his or her genitals, make sure that what you are doing is pleasurable: ask if she or he would like you to do something different.

Cup your hand and use vibratory movements on the vulva

PLEASURING A MAN

Start by squeezing his testes very gently and running your fingers up and down the length of his penis. Pay attention to the glans and the frenulum and gradually make your hand movements more rhythmic.

PLEASURING A WOMAN

Gently explore the vaginal entrance and the perineum before you begin to stimulate her clitoris. Light pressure and circular movements will increase arousal. Once she is lubricated, give her regular, rhythmical stimulation.

ORAL SEX

Extremely intimate and erotic, oral sex is very pleasurable to both partners. The tongue and mouth are softer and more versatile than the fingers, and are capable of producing wide-ranging sensual experiences, which often result in heightened orgasms.

FELLATIO
Performed by women on men, kissing, licking, and sucking of the penis, done rhythmically, may lead to orgasm.

PRELIMINARIES
Start off by gently kissing and licking his body, hovering tantalizingly close to the genital region.

TAKING CARE
Once you take his penis into your mouth, your saliva will act as a natural lubricant and, as long as you cover your teeth with your lips and take care not to bite, there is no danger of hurting your partner.

INCREASING SENSATION

As he becomes more aroused, use your mouth and tongue to explore the head, glans, and ridge of the penis. Vary your tongue strokes and lick the underside of the penis, paying particular attention to the frenulum. When your partner is highly excited, move your head up and down in a steady rhythm.

If you don't want him to ejaculate in your mouth, withdraw, and use your hand or switch to intercourse

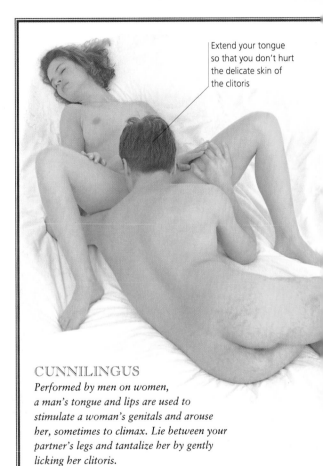

Extend your tongue so that you don't hurt the delicate skin of the clitoris

CUNNILINGUS

Performed by men on women, a man's tongue and lips are used to stimulate a woman's genitals and arouse her, sometimes to climax. Lie between your partner's legs and tantalize her by gently licking her clitoris.

AROUSING YOUR PARTNER

Spend some time licking, sucking, and nuzzling her clitoris and labia, sometimes penetrating the vagina with the tip of your tongue.

THE 69 POSITION

Lying mouth-to-genitals allows partners to lick and suck each other at the same time. Some couples find that this mutual pleasuring adds to their excitement, others find it interferes with pleasure and feel it is better to concentrate on each other one at a time.

SEXY GAMES

Foreplay needs to be stimulating and arousing, particularly in a long-standing relationship, where repetitive behaviour can easily become a turn-off. Heighten sexual tension and enhance lovemaking by engaging in varied activities that have an erotic edge. You can tease and tantalize your partner in many different ways – the only proviso being that you both enjoy what is happening.

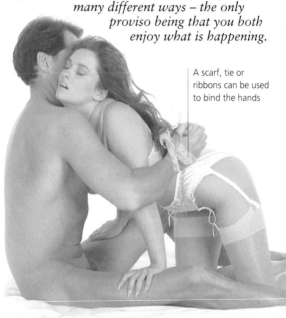

A scarf, tie or ribbons can be used to bind the hands

CLOTHED OR NAKED

Insisting that one partner remains clothed while the other is naked will promote eroticism. It can be incredibly sexy to insert your hand underneath garments or press fabric against the skin.

BLINDFOLDING

Increase your partner's sexual tension by giving caresses that are anticipated even though they can't be seen before being enjoyed.

TEASING RESTRAINT

Rendering your partner incapable of action is titillating in the extreme. Use a soft scarf or tie to bind your partner's hands, then insinuate your provocatively clad body against his or hers.

ROLE PLAYING

Although it's not necessary to use a lot of props when engaging in sexy games with your partner, dressing up can make some games more realistic and thus more exciting. Dressing the part can inspire imaginative scenarios. Don't feel obliged to go to the trouble of donning a French maid's costume or a uniform because everyday clothes can often be used to good effect, particularly if, for example, you play at being the sophisticated seducer to your partner's naive virgin.

VAMP IT UP
Dress up in skintight clothes that show the shape of your body, but do not reveal much bare skin. Treat your partner to a special seduction routine; take control and make sure you initiate all the action.

TAKE THINGS SLOWLY
Treat her gently but firmly; it helps if she makes a play of slightly resisting your caresses. Keep your movements slow and erotic; don't let her rush you. Look at her body as if it were completely new to you; make her feel as though it were.

BE IN CONTROL

Remove her garments one at
a time when you feel you've
"won" through; don't let
her help. You should be
persuasive, pushy, and
penetrating as you
make love, making
her feel as though
she's discovering sex
for the first time.

Ensure each
movement is
charged with
sensuality

PLAY WITH
EXPECTATIONS

The most important part of
your seduction routine is the
element of anticipation. Keep
thwarting his expectations
by moving your hands close
to his penis and then away
again. Even when you are
stimulating him, use this
stop-and-start technique to
create new levels of arousal.
Tease him, too, by pre-
tending not to be aroused.

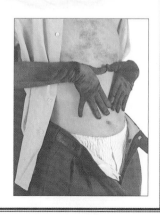

FANTASIES

Although it's not always easy to act out some of your sexual fantasies, they can add spice to your sex life and inject energy into your relationship. As long as your partner agrees and no one is hurt, the only limit is your imagination.

FANTASY FEMALE

She is young, sexually insatiable and experienced, readily available, and looks the part.

MALE FANTASIES

These often involve sexually experienced partners who may indulge in meting out "punishment".

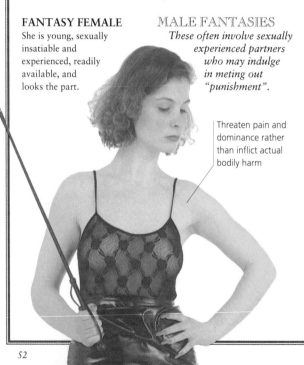

Threaten pain and dominance rather than inflict actual bodily harm

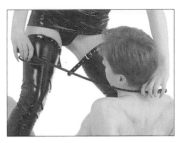

"FORCING" OBEDIENCE

You can use a riding crop or whip to threaten your partner into assuming positions that make you the dominant figure.

THE PLEASURE OF PAIN

Although you are playing a psychological game, partners can make it realistic by dressing up and using props. Thongs, whips, and blindfolds will "unman" him and make your partner your slave – to do with as you wish.

Leather combined with lace intimidates and invites

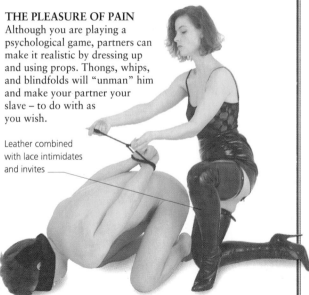

FEMALE FANTASIES

Anonymity is important in many female fantasies. The idea of making love to a stranger or dream lover enables a woman to inject variety into her sex life without threatening a long-standing relationship.

FANTASY MALE

A partner can play on the female fantasy of being made love to in the darkness by a stranger. Begin your seduction routine by going up behind your partner when she is naked. Put one hand softly over her eyes and use the other to caress her.

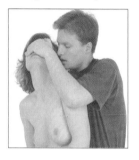

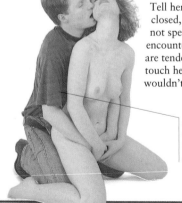

KEEP HER GUESSING

Tell her to keep her eyes closed, but otherwise do not speak throughout the encounter. Use actions that are tender yet firm, and touch her in a way that you wouldn't usually.

Add to the feeling of spontaneity by keeping your clothes on

chapter three

VARIATIONS ON MAKING LOVE

MAN-ON-TOP POSITIONS

The most well-known of these couplings is the missionary position. It is popular because it allows the man complete freedom of movement, the opportunity of easily assuming other poses without withdrawing, and maintenance of eye contact with his partner.

MISSIONARY
The man lies between his partner's thighs. He is the active partner as she has little freedom of movement.

RAISED BOTTOM
Pillows are used under the woman's hips in this variation of the missionary position. Raising her bottom allows slightly deeper penetration because the pelvis is tilted and the vagina is more accessible.

Spreading your legs apart will allow your partner to penetrate more deeply

HIP ROTATION

Here, the woman can tense her buttocks, and lift and swivel her hips while thrusting upwards. This may trigger orgasm quickly.

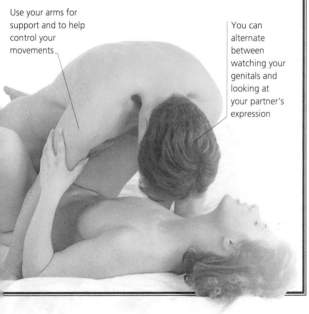

Use your arms for support and to help control your movements

You can alternate between watching your genitals and looking at your partner's expression

LEGS RAISED

By varying the position of her legs, the woman will ensure a variety of sensations. Drawing them up closer to her chest, for example, will change the angle at which her partner can enter her. The more supple she is, the easier she will find it to move from one position to the other. She can begin in this position and move on to the feet-on-shoulders position, although she needs to be quite flexible for the latter.

Press down on his buttocks to lift yourself

FEET ON SHOULDERS

This allows the man to penetrate his partner to the maximum. She should be fully aroused, however, so that her vagina has reached its full length.

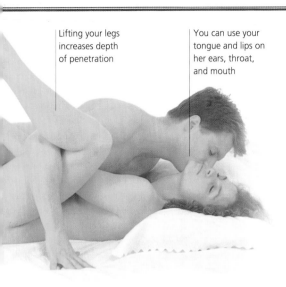

Lifting your legs increases depth of penetration

You can use your tongue and lips on her ears, throat, and mouth

SPLIT LEVELS

The woman lies on the bed with her legs raised and the man assumes a semi-crouching position on the floor close to the bed. When he penetrates his

partner, his penis is parallel to her vagina, and this produces a slightly different sensation from that experienced with the usual downward-thrusting angle.

WOMAN-ON-TOP POSITIONS

While allowing the woman a more active role in lovemaking, these positions also feed a man's need sometimes to take a more passive role during sex. The woman can choose the type and speed of movement that is most satisfying, as well as the depth of penetration.

REVERSE MISSIONARY

The woman can raise and lower herself on her partner's penis to bring on orgasm. If she moves backwards and forwards, this will provide friction to the vaginal walls and clitoris.

Use your hands to lift yourself up

ON KNEES
By raising herself and resting on her knees, the woman changes the sensations for both partners.

FACING AWAY
With her back to her partner, it is easier for a woman to fantasize about what she is doing (and with whom!). The woman can move backwards and forwards very easily and she can stimulate herself by hand if she wants to. Many men are quite turned on by bottoms, and this position gives the man an unparalleled view.

LYING ON TOP

Both partners' pubic regions are perfectly aligned and she can rock from side to side or move backwards and forwards for stimulation.

THE "FROG" POSITION

If the woman lies with her legs on top of her partner's, she can use her feet and hands to raise and lower herself. She is free to move while the man is freed from being active.

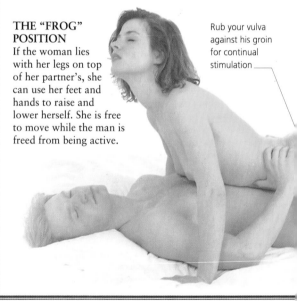

Rub your vulva against his groin for continual stimulation

LYING IN-BETWEEN HIS LEGS

Here, the man's penis is tightly squeezed between his partner's thighs, which is very pleasurable for him. Although the woman cannot move freely, the shaft of the penis should stimulate her clitoris. This is a good position to lie in after ejaculation because it is comfortable and intimate and allows partners to kiss and caress each other.

Use his feet to push off against

SIDE-BY-SIDE POSITIONS

These couplings score highly for bodily contact and freedom of movement. The "spoons" position, in particular, is a gentle and relaxing way of making love.

FACE TO FACE
You can roll over to face each other from a man- or woman-on-top position. To achieve deeper penetration, the woman should bend her leg and rest it on the man's legs.

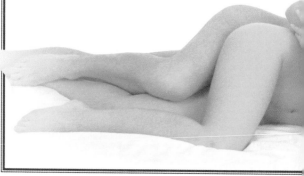

MAN BEHIND

The woman rolls on to her hip to make penetration easier. Her partner has access to her breasts and vagina so that a great deal of intimacy and touching is possible, although penile stimulation of the clitoris is low.

Bend your knees to make penetration more comfortable

THE "SPOONS" POSITION

The woman lies on her side with her knees up, while the man follows the contours of her body with his own. He is free to caress his partner's upper body and kiss the back of her neck while being able to reach her vagina.

You can reach around to caress your partner's breasts and nipples

CLASPED LEGS

Partners lie face-to-face in a close embrace. The woman clasps her partner around the waist with her legs; he can keep his legs straight or one leg slightly bent (above). However, if he pushes his leg up (below), he can achieve a greater depth of penetration and may find it easier to thrust.
Partners will enjoy the physical and emotional intimacy of this pose.

Draw your knees up high to clasp your partner's hips

LYING WITH LEGS RAISED

The woman can lift her legs over the man's hip, so that he can reach down and insert his penis into her vagina in a gentle way. To keep his penis there, the woman should hold her legs tightly closed.

Move your leg up and down to change the depth of penetration

BACK APPROACH

Because the man moves very little, it is easy for him to control his orgasm. The woman will benefit from G-spot stimulation.

Push against her body to achieve the desired depth of penetration

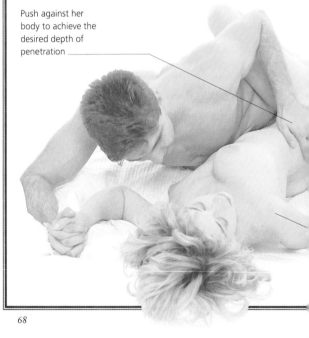

Move your thigh gently against her vulva

WOMAN LYING FLAT

The woman turns on to her back and opens her legs wide. Her partner insinuates one leg between hers so that her vulva receives more stimulation on penetration. He will find the sensations different too.

ADVANCED SIDE-TO-SIDE

Where partners are fairly athletic, a front-facing position can be altered so that the woman, while keeping one leg on her partner's hip, angles away from him. He then uses her body to push against to achieve maximum genital contact.

You can lie back and enjoy the sensations

SITTING POSITIONS

Although sitting positions are not the fastest way to reach orgasm, they promote intimacy and closeness because of their symmetrical, face-to-face nature. Neither partner is required to take the dominant role.

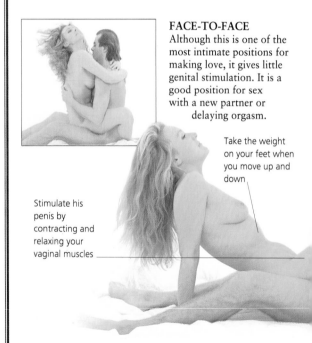

FACE-TO-FACE
Although this is one of the most intimate positions for making love, it gives little genital stimulation. It is a good position for sex with a new partner or delaying orgasm.

Take the weight on your feet when you move up and down

Stimulate his penis by contracting and relaxing your vaginal muscles

SITTING ASTRIDE

Though the man's movements are restricted, the woman can press the whole of her upper body against her partner's and provide genital stimulation by moving up and down.

LEANING APART

You can assume this position initially, in which case the woman's hips must be above the man's, or take up the position from a woman-on-top one. In this case, the woman needs to draw up her knees so that she is crouching over her partner before she slips her legs behind his back. He can then straighten up and support his partner. By leaning back and taking the weight on their hands, partners have a greater opportunity to move and to watch each other's reactions.

SEATED FACE-TO-FACE

Here, you have the intimacy of being very close, but, because you are on a chair, you have greater freedom to move. If you are supple you can make this position part of a sequence: from sitting, move to a standing position, and then to a kneeling position. Finish in a man-on-top position.

SEATED SIDEWAYS-ON

If the woman turns to the side on the chair, she makes her genital area more available for manual stimulation by herself or her partner. Internally, she should still keep hold of her partner's penis.

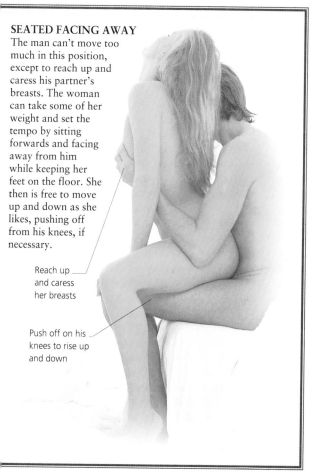

SEATED FACING AWAY

The man can't move too
much in this position,
except to reach up and
caress his partner's
breasts. The woman
can take some of her
weight and set the
tempo by sitting
forwards and facing
away from him
while keeping her
feet on the floor. She
then is free to move
up and down as she
likes, pushing off
from his knees, if
necessary.

Reach up
and caress
her breasts

Push off on his
knees to rise up
and down

KNEELING POSITIONS

Usually achieved from a standing, sitting, or man-on-top position, you can adopt kneeling positions during sex to vary the pace and sensation.

Use your arm for support and to push up against your partner

Grasp her underneath her buttocks

RAISED BOTTOM

The woman lies back and hooks her legs around her partner's torso while he penetrates her. The man grasps her sides to lift her up and change the angle and depth of penetration.

SUPPORTED KNEELING

Although this position is easy to adopt, it can be hard to keep up for any length of time. Use it as a transitional position in a sequence from a standing or kneeling position to a man-on-top position. The man should face his partner straight on, then insert his penis into her vagina. Once inside, he should draw up his partner on to his body, so that he is supporting most of her weight with his arms and knees.

Hold up your partner on your thighs

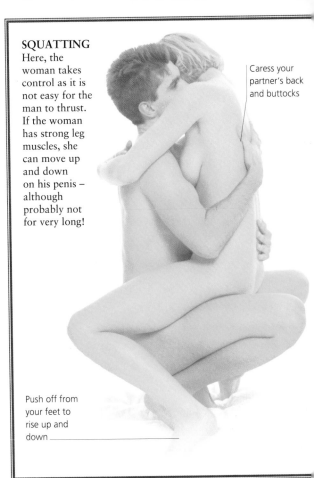

SQUATTING

Here, the woman takes control as it is not easy for the man to thrust. If the woman has strong leg muscles, she can move up and down on his penis – although probably not for very long!

Caress your partner's back and buttocks

Push off from your feet to rise up and down

UPRIGHT KNEELING
By keeping her feet on the ground, the woman can rock her pelvis up and down to stimulate the man. He can hold her around the waist to guide her movements.

PARALLEL BODIES
Both partners should kneel on a soft surface. Then the woman slides forwards, opening her thighs, to sit on her partner's lap. Alternatively, the man can insinuate himself underneath his partner during penetration. This position is low on genital stimulation, but good for upper-body contact and kissing.

CHAIR SUPPORT

Support can make kneeling positions more comfortable. Use a chair or couch that is not too high. The woman should sit, clasping her partner around the waist with her legs while he penetrates her. Alternatively, the woman can lie on a table and her partner can enter her from a standing position.

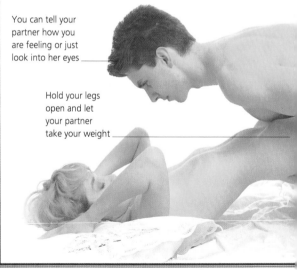

You can tell your partner how you are feeling or just look into her eyes

Hold your legs open and let your partner take your weight

RAISED LEGS

The woman rests one or both of her legs against the man's chest and shoulders while he grips her thighs. The tighter she holds her thighs together, the tighter the woman can grip the man's penis. The man should alternate light, shallow strokes with deep, penetrating ones.

ARCHED BACK

This is another position in which the man can thrust deeply. The woman can arch her body, offering up her vagina to be penetrated, or the man can penetrate his partner and, supporting her underneath her buttocks, subsequently raise her on to his thighs. From there, he can rock her up and down against him. It is a very provocative position but ‑is probably most easily achieved by a supple and flexible woman.

STANDING POSITIONS

Very good for impromptu lovemaking when you don't want to lie down or undress fully, standing positions do, however, require that partners be somewhat athletic. The man can lift his partner on to him or he can penetrate her from behind while they are both standing.

FULL LIFT
An athletic man can lift up his partner so that she is fully supported. The woman can help pull herself up by clasping her partner's shoulders and using her legs to climb up his hips. A wall can be used to provide leverage.

Embrace him tightly to maintain your hold

Use thigh pressure to grasp his hips

Balance the weight between both feet

FACE-TO-FACE
Most successful and effective when both partners are of similar height, this position permits extensive genital stimulation, although penetration tends to be rather shallow.

CROUCHING LIFT
Unless the woman is considerably smaller than her partner, the man will have to adjust his position in order for her weight to be evenly distributed and supported. He should stand with legs bent; she can help by crossing her legs behind her partner's back.

Bringing your legs behind his back will help distribute your weight

BACK PLAY

When the man stands behind his partner, the alteration in body position makes new areas of stimulation accessible, and transforms even standard caresses into something more exciting for both the man and woman. The back of the woman's neck becomes more available to her partner, who should also reach around to caress her breasts and clitoris. The woman can rub her buttocks seductively against his body.

WOMAN BENT OVER

Penetration is deep while the man enjoys complete freedom of movement. This position is thrilling for many women because it provides intense stimulation of the front wall of the vagina.

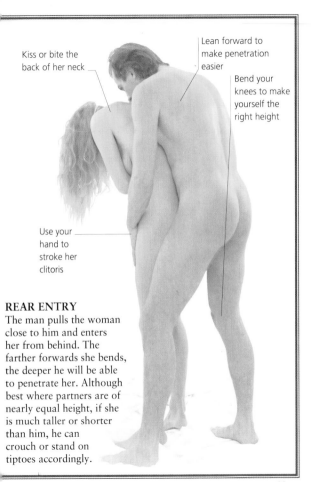

Kiss or bite the
back of her neck

Lean forward to
make penetration
easier

Bend your
knees to make
yourself the
right height

Use your
hand to
stroke her
clitoris

REAR ENTRY

The man pulls the woman
close to him and enters
her from behind. The
farther forwards she bends,
the deeper he will be able
to penetrate her. Although
best where partners are of
nearly equal height, if she
is much taller or shorter
than him, he can
crouch or stand on
tiptoes accordingly.

REAR-ENTRY POSITIONS

Penetration from behind can be in a standing, sitting, kneeling, or lying position and it doesn't have to mean that the man is dominant. There are several positions in which the woman can take the lead and control the sexual tempo.

LYING FLAT
The woman can arch her back and raise her body or she can lie flat. She can have her legs together or spread apart.

THE "DOGGIE" POSITION
The man can penetrate deeply in this position and has complete freedom to move. Some women find being penetrated from behind highly arousing; others feel vulnerable.

LAP SITTING

The woman lowers herself on to the man's penis when he is seated, helping to support herself with her arms. As with all rear-entry positions, the woman receives intense stimulation of the front wall of the vagina.

Move yourself up and down on his penis

You can help support her under the thighs

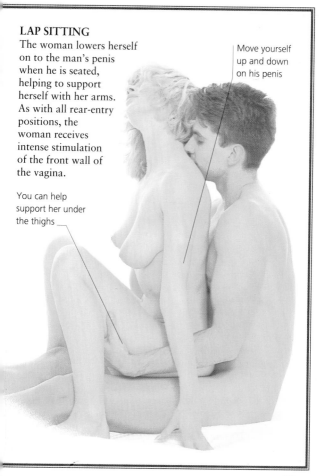

UPRIGHT "DOGGIE"

Rather than resting on the floor, the woman supports herself on a surface such as a bed or chair. The penis is still naturally aligned with the vagina, but the man is better able to caress his partner's breasts.

You are free to initiate movements

You can thrust fully, letting your fantasies take over

SUPPORTED "DOGGIE"

This position is good on the bed or floor. Soft pillows will help take some of the woman's weight and, by opening her legs wide, she can present her upturned vagina invitingly.

MAN ON TOP

Rear-entry positions encourage female fantasies, as being taken from behind is arousing for many women. Men also will enjoy the novelty this approach provides in terms of dominance, sensation, and visual stimulation.

You may find the vulnerability of the position, and the opportunity it gives to fantasize, very exciting

ADVANCED POSITIONS

Sexual experimentation is worthwhile for a number of reasons. For example, if sex is to remain fulfilling and stimulating, it needs to be varied, and sometimes physical conditions or partner preference require changes to routine techniques. These more athletic postures can provide new and exciting sensations, as long as both partners are fit.

SIDEWAYS-ON

Starting from a woman-on-top position, the woman can carefully back away from her partner, until she is sitting between his legs. If she is agile, she can ensure his penis remains inside.

You can be the more active partner in many advanced positions

The success of this position depends on your agility

THE "CRAB"
The woman sits astride her partner while facing away; once his penis is inside her vagina, she leans backwards.

If the penis slips out, you can reach down and masturbate your partner

WOMAN ON TOP
The woman can set the tempo and pace of lovemaking by assuming a more active, freer posture. She can experiment with positional changes, arching her body backwards and pressing her legs close against her partner's flank, while using her hands and arms for support.

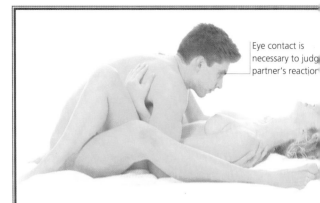

Eye contact is
necessary to judge
partner's reaction

MAN ABOVE
Starting from an on-top position, he brings his legs
forwards and sits up. While his thrusting is curtailed, his
partner can more easily rub her vulva against his groin.

SUPPORTED KNEELING
From an on-top position, the man grasps his partner
firmly and, as he moves gradually into a kneeling
position, he arches her legs off the bed and on to
his thighs. The woman can help by supporting
herself with her arm thrown around her
partner's neck.

PRESS-UPS
Good for controlling ejaculation, the woman can relax completely while the man sets the pace.

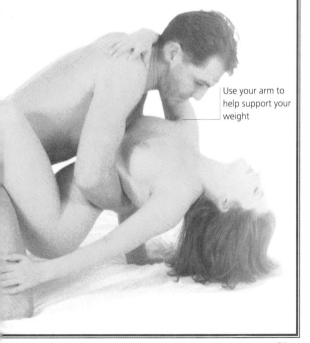

Use your arm to help support your weight

"SCISSORS"
This variation of a woman-on-top position is good for manual stimulation of the clitoris.

RAISED "DOGGIE"
The man can enter the woman from a standing position or after she has bent over. To make the coupling more successful, the woman can raise herself on pillows or the man can bend his knees.

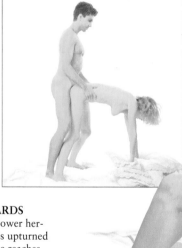

SITTING BACKWARDS
An agile woman can lower herself on to her partner's upturned thighs. Once there, she reaches down to insert his penis. She then can raise or lower herself on it, or provide stimulation by moving from side to side.

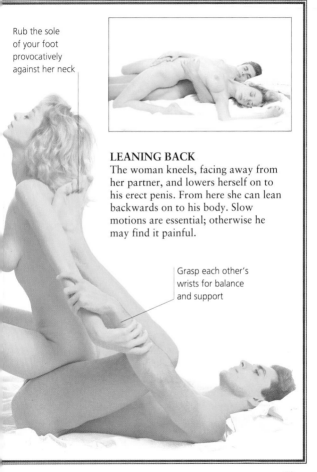

Rub the sole
of your foot
provocatively
against her neck

LEANING BACK

The woman kneels, facing away from
her partner, and lowers herself on to
his erect penis. From here she can lean
backwards on to his body. Slow
motions are essential; otherwise he
may find it painful.

Grasp each other's
wrists for balance
and support

TANTRIC SEX

The Eastern philosophy of Tantra is concerned with heightening and prolonging sexual arousal. Its main components are sensuous stroking, which helps you focus on your partner's body and your own reactions, and very slow intercourse – with the penis alternately penetrating and withdrawing from the vagina.

REAR ENTRY

In this position, the man can easily control the force and depth of his penetration. Also, he can masturbate his partner to orgasm when he is ready for his final climax, at which time her contractions will provide the impetus for his own orgasm.

Enter and withdraw from your partner often, but slowly

94

MISSIONARY POSITION

The man can prevent himself ejaculating too soon by gently pulling down his testicles or pressing his frenulum.

Move slowly and sensuously at all times

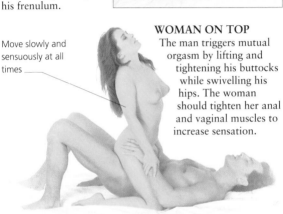

WOMAN ON TOP

The man triggers mutual orgasm by lifting and tightening his buttocks while swivelling his hips. The woman should tighten her anal and vaginal muscles to increase sensation.

SIDE-BY-SIDE

In this position, the man can penetrate shallowly without thrusting. The penis rests against the clitoris between insertions.

INDEX

A
Advanced positions, 88
Arousal, female, 8
  male, 10

B
Blindfolding, 49
Body paint, 37
Breasts, 31
Brushes, 36

C
Circumcision, 12
Clitoris, 14
Condoms, 18
Cunnilingus, 46

D
Detumescence, 11
"Doggie" positions,
  raised, 92
  rear entry, 84
  supported, 87
  upright, 86

E
Edibles, 37
Erogenous zones, 30
Erotic enhancers, 36

F
Fantasies, female, 54
  male, 52
Fellatio, 44
French kissing, 32
"Frog" position, 62

G
Games, sexy, 48
Genitals, 30
  clitoris, 14
  penis, 12
  vagina, 15
  G-spot, 16

K
Kissing, 32
Kneeling positions,
  74
  supported, 90

M
Man-on-top
  positions, 56
  advanced, 90
  rear entry, 87
  Tantric sex, 95
Masks, 37
Massage, 38
  sharing a, 40
Masturbation,
  female, 24
  male, 22
  mutual, 42
Missionary positions,
  56
  reverse, 60
  Tantric sex, 95

O
Orgasm, female, 9
  male, 11
Oral sex, 44

P
Penis, 12
Push-up position, 91

R
Rear-entry positions,
  84
  standing, 83
  Tantric sex, 94
Resolution (female), 9
Role playing, 50

S
Safer sex, 18
"Scissors" position,
  92
Sensual massage, 38

Sex organs,
  female, 14
  male, 12
Sexual response,
  female, 8
  male, 10
Sexy games, 48
  undressing, 28
Side-by-side
  positions, 64
  Tantric sex, 95
Sitting positions, 70
  advanced, 92
"Spoons" position,
  65
Squatting position, 76
Standing positions,
  80
Stimulation,
  clitoral, 24
  female body, 25
  G-spot, 16, 17
  male body, 23
  visual, 28
Stroking, 34

T
Tantric sex, 94
Teasing restraint, 49
Touching, 34

U
Undressing, 28
Using a condom, 20
Using a vibrator, 26

V
Vagina, 15
Vibrators, 26

W
Woman-on-top
  positions 60
  advanced, 89
  "scissors," 92
  Tantric sex, 95